The Problem of t
in Tudor a
Early Stuart England

IN THE SAME SERIES

Austin Woolrych
England without a King 1649–1660

E. J. Evans
The Great Reform Act of 1832

P. M. Harman
The Scientific Revolution

J. M. MacKenzie
The Partition of Africa

J. H. Shennan
France before the Revolution

LANCASTER PAMPHLETS

The Problem of the Poor in Tudor and Early Stuart England

A. L. Beier

METHUEN · LONDON AND NEW YORK

First published in 1983 by
Methuen & Co. Ltd
11 New Fetter Lane,
London EC4P 4EE

Published in the USA by
Methuen & Co.
in association with Methuen, Inc.
733 Third Avenue, New York,
NY 10017

Typeset in Great Britain by
Scarborough Typesetting Services
and printed by
Richard Clay (The Chaucer Press)
Bungay, Suffolk

British Library Cataloguing in
Publication Data

Beier, A. L.
The problem of the poor in Tudor
and early Stuart England.
– (Lancaster pamphlets)
1. Poor – England – History
2. Public welfare – England – History
I. Title   II. Series
362.5' 8' 094   HV 245

ISBN 0–416–35060–7

Contents

Foreword   vii

Acknowledgements   ix

Introduction   1

Medieval origins   2

Hard times, 1500–1650   4

The response   13

Perceptions of poverty   13
Unofficial charity   19
State poor-relief   23
'Masterless men'   29

Conclusion   36

Bibliography   37

Appendix: Provisions of Tudor
and Early Stuart poor-laws   39

Foreword

Lancaster Pamphlets offer concise and up-to-date accounts of major historical topics, primarily for the help of students preparing for Advanced Level examinations, though they should also be of value to those pursuing introductory courses in universities and other institutions of higher education. They do not rely on prior textbook knowledge. Without being all-embracing, their aims are to bring some of the central themes or problems confronting students and teachers into sharper focus than the textbook writer can hope to do; to provide the reader with some of the results of recent research which the textbook may not embody; and to stimulate thought about the whole interpretation of the topic under discussion.

At the end of this pamphlet is a numbered list of the recent or fairly recent works that the writer considers most relevant to his subject. Where a statement or a paragraph is particularly indebted to one or more of these works, the number is given in the text in brackets. This serves to show readers where they may find a more detailed exposition of the point concerned.

Acknowledgements

I wish to record my thanks to two members of my department, Eric Evans and David King, for their comments on the first draft of this pamphlet; to N. P. Webb and Julian Hill for permission to cite evidence from their theses; and to Rosemary Fenton for typing a final draft in the nick of time. As always, my greatest debt is to my family.

The Problem of the Poor in Tudor and Early Stuart England

Introduction

From 1485 to 1649 Parliament passed over two dozen statutes dealing with the poor. The legislation did not cease, moreover, with the fall of Charles I. Social security and unemployment benefits are foundation-stones of British society today, and only recently have the nineteenth-century vagrancy laws been repealed. But the Tudor and early Stuart poor-laws are not simply a series of Acts of Parliament, numerous, wordy and difficult to recall in examinations. Like other events in history, they must be viewed with reference to their 'lives and times'. So one aim of this pamphlet is to place the legislation in its historical context: in relation to earlier, medieval facilities for handling poverty; by examining the questions, 'who were the poor, and how numerous were they?'; and by showing the influence of economic conditions, of ideas concerning poverty, and of the interests of those who ruled.

But history involves interpreting the facts as well as describing them, and so we shall refer to certain schools of thought on the poor-laws. First, there is the 'state-building' view. This approach sees the legislation as an early stage in the growth of a welfare state, reaching its peak under the early Stuarts and then declining, to the detriment of the poor (13, 23). Second, there is the position

1

that a 'Protestant ethic' was crucial in the treatment of the poor. One version of this interpretation is that Protestants took a uniquely harsh stance towards them, leading to statutory discrimination between those able and those unfit to work [20]. A refinement of this view argues that to the 'deserving', at least, Protestants were extraordinarily generous with charity; so much so that the poor-laws were redundant except in emergencies [11]. Historians have also stressed the role of economic and social changes in triggering official concern about the poor between 1500 and 1650: population growth, rising prices, falling wages, agrarian dislocation, migration and urbanization. The lot of the poor worsened under these pressures, it is thought [15].

However, mass distress did not begin or end with changes of regime like those of 1485 and 1649; nor with alterations in the official faith; nor with the shifting sands of economic fluctuations. What was mainly involved were two variables: the appearance of great numbers of propertyless persons, and the authorities' reactions to them. Destitution certainly worsened under the Tudors and early Stuarts, but it is simplistic to impose precise dates on the problem, which even today remains a cause of discontent.

Medieval origins

Official concern about the needy and unemployed dates not from Tudor times, but from the Middle Ages. This is not surprising, for the two periods shared certain features of pre-industrial societies that made poverty common rather than exceptional. Human and animal power were the main sources of energy, and production was subject to myriad constraints: night and day, bad weather, and diseases (of man and beast). Another hindrance was that, because of high birth- and death-rates, a large share of the population were unemployable. The proportion of children was perhaps twice as high as today, which meant fewer productive adults than in an industrialized society. Short life-expectancy had the same result, as well as leaving many orphans and widows [5]. Finally, wealth was unequally distributed, with a small minority of lords, merchants and rich peasants in possession of the lion's share.

Medieval society experienced a number of disturbing changes from about 1200. First, rising population levels and increased exactions by lords spelt harder times for tenants. Second, towns grew both in number and in size. City air might make one free of servile bonds, but it could also make one poor. As centres of industry, towns contained hundreds, sometimes thousands of process-workers, who mostly lived on a knife-edge of poverty. The final blow was the liberation of labour from bonds of serfdom. The labour shortage caused by the Black Death, combined with migration and struggles against lords for freedom, meant that by 1500 formal serfdom was almost a dead letter.

Medieval society developed a number of institutions to deal with these upheavals. From the twelfth century canon lawyers revivified legislation requiring parish care for the indigent. In some villages manorial custom provided for the helpless and landless. Another defence was the 'parish stock' (often a flock of sheep or herd of cattle), the profits of which were directed to the relief of the poor. Parish guilds, to which almost all householders belonged, acted as mutual-aid societies (22).

Medieval towns also developed facilities for poor-relief. Craft guilds came to the aid of members in distress and endowed almshouses and hospitals. The numbers of hospitals reached a peak of nearly 700 between 1216 and 1350. Although not 'hospitals' in our sense, they included facilities for the care of the diseased, as well as almshouses and lodgings for travellers (7). Finally, some towns acted to relieve the needy, running hospitals, storing supplies of corn, and levying poor-rates. In addition to institutional relief there was a great deal of charity. After all, the Church's doctrine held that 'good works' helped to aid the soul's passage from Purgatory to Heaven. Finally, there was a considerable corpus of medieval vagrancy legislation. Before 1300 it mainly covered runaway serfs, but from that date was directed against disorderly and criminal groups, and after 1350 against labourers who refused to work for statutory wages or who begged. The appearance of a criminal underworld at this time is not surprising, for social problems were mounting in town and country from about 1250. In seeking to control labour the state

3

regulated the poor generally. The Statute of Labourers of 1349 restrained alms-giving, particularly hand-outs to able-bodied beggars, so that 'they may be compelled to labour'. In some measure, therefore, there existed 'medieval poor-laws'.

Hard times, 1500–1650

The fullest development of the poor-laws nevertheless began in the sixteenth century. From the 1530s the system was transformed. The change came not overnight in a 'revolution in government', but over several decades. By the early seventeenth century it is possible to speak of a national poor-law system in England, perhaps Europe's first. Indeed, by the end of the century the cost of relief provoked a national debate involving some of the leading minds of the age. By that time the country had seen vast institutional upheavals. Parliament had taken on the responsibility of the relief of the disabled. It passed laws that gradually imposed compulsory poor-rates on every parish in the land and required the appointment of new, secular officials to administer them. Even the monarch and the Privy Council became active in regulating the poor. Moreover, towns began to take independent action to handle the problem, often anticipating moves by central government. They made censuses of the poor, levied compulsory rates, and devised work-projects for the unemployed. But before discussing these dramatic changes, we must establish the context in which they occurred.

Perhaps the most striking feature of society's structure on the eve of the Reformation was the great mass of the poor and vulnerable. This meant that when things got worse, as they certainly did from 1500 to 1650, there were multitudes who had little to fall back on; who possessed, in one writer's words, 'no property at all beyond the clothes they stood up in, the tools of their trade, and a few sticks of furniture' (10). It was to support this considerable group, to stop them from starving and, worse, rioting, that the poor-laws were passed.

Contemporary observers were convinced the numbers of the poor were enormous, estimating them as a quarter to a half of the

4

population. Reliable taxation records suggest that a third to a half lived in or near poverty in the 1520s and again in the 1670s. Towards the end of the period Gregory King put the total 'decreasing the wealth of the kingdom' as high as three-fifths. Thus England began the Tudor and ended the Stuart age with a great army of needy persons, possibly the majority of the country's inhabitants.

Who were the poor? Statutes distinguished the disabled and the able-bodied, but it was more complicated than that. Instead we may divide them into the *settled* and the *vagrant* poor, contrasting groups receiving different treatment. The first were eligible for relief under the poor laws, but the second were treated as criminals. In reality, even this distinction is somewhat artificial, for the 'settled' easily slipped into vagrancy. But to the authorities the difference was important, for the resident poor might swell the poor-rates, while vagrants had no entitlement to relief. Moreover, the latter were considered greater threats to property and public order. The numbers of the settled poor varied according to time and place, generally ranging from a fifth to a third of the population. Of course their numbers rose when times were bad. In Warwick in 1587 those requiring relief doubled after a poor harvest. The stationary poor tended to live in suburbs, where rents were low, on rural wastelands, and in forests. They had smaller households than the better-off, because they could not afford to keep as many children and servants. Despite the label 'settled', local pauper populations were volatile: 50 per cent of Warwick's poor disappeared in just five years in the 1580s through death or migration. Women were especially common, outnumbering men by two to one and heading households in a majority of cases. By contrast, in the population generally, women were in a bare majority and were household heads in just one in six instances (2). The ages of the sedentary poor suggest there were three phases to poverty: first in childhood and early adolescence (up to age 16) before the young left home for service; then as an adult aged from 30 to 60 when people married, had children, and before the latter left the household; and finally as an old person over 60, when the poor were often listed as 'impotent' and 'unable to labour'. Up to 70 per cent of Elizabethan and early

5

Stuart settled paupers were able-bodied, judging by censuses, but often unemployed. If they found work at all, it was in the poorer trades, especially in the cloth industry.

There are no accurate figures for the vagrant poor because they were obviously difficult to count. Again, contemporaries thought their numbers were great and growing. In reality they were certainly smaller in number than the settled poor. For what it is worth, at least 26,000 were arrested in the 1630s, or roughly 0.5 per cent of the country's population. But this figure is probably on the low side, since many no doubt escaped capture. It was not just vagrants' numbers, though, that worried officials. Rather it was their disruption of the labour system and political order. Perhaps most disturbing was the fact that they were mainly recruited among the lowest paid (yet most numerous) groups of wage-earners. Above all, they were dependent workers, that is, servants and apprentices, who formed the bulk of the labour-force in early modern England. If they were idle, production in all sectors would grind to a halt, and unimaginable disorders might ensue (1, 18).

A number of other occupations came under the vagrancy laws because they were thought potentially to threaten the state. These included such diverse groups as pedlars, ex-soldiers and mariners, entertainers, students and wizards. Governments required them to carry licences, if they tolerated them at all. In contrast to the sedentary poor, vagrants were mainly male, especially adolescents and young adults, as in ghettos today. Hence frequent reference to them as 'sturdy' and 'lusty', and the official perception of them as dangerous. Finally, vagabonds were footloose and perpetrated a variety of crimes. Only a minority reported any settled 'home'. On average they covered 70 to 80 miles a month, living in ale-houses, sleeping rough, begging, working and stealing. Next to vagrancy, their most common offence was indeed larceny, although a minority committed more serious misdeeds including burglary and highway robbery. Another small minority spread sedition and slander, or were religious dissidents. But fundamentally vagrants were more likely to be cast-offs from unstable master/servant relationships than hardened members of an 'underworld'.

The poor unquestionably got poorer between 1500 and 1650, and without government intervention might have threatened the social order. The list of 'bread and butter' problems facing them in the period is long. The country's population increased from perhaps 2.3 million in 1520 to 4.8 million in 1630. Even though pre-Black Death levels were not reached until the early Stuart years, and the country was at most a tenth as densely populated as today, growth still posed problems. Obviously if the poor simply reproduced as fast as the rest of society, their needs would have doubled. But sheer weight of numbers is not the whole explanation of their difficulties. Other things considered, their share of the population was probably greater by 1650 than a century before, because of the peculiar character of the rise in numbers. It was a high birth-rate rather than a decline in mortality that fuelled the rise. In other words, the period saw a 'baby-boom' such as occurred after the Second World War, but in this case lasting for nearly two centuries. The high birth-rate, despite high infant and child mortality, meant that the problem noted earlier of large numbers of unproductive youngsters was exacerbated. Tudor and early Stuart England unquestionably had a 'youth problem' of far greater dimensions than Britain today. In our day similar conditions can really only be observed in Third World countries. Much poor-law legislation was directed at controlling this group.

If 50 to 60 per cent of the population were unable to support themselves, how did they live? The short answer is badly, and grinding poverty was undoubtedly the lot of many. But in fact we know extremely little about how the poor lived: their housing, diet, health-care, sources of income, beliefs and expectations. The indirect signs nevertheless suggest hard times from 1500 to 1650. Take prices and wages. Although price rises averaging about 4 per cent a year for consumables may fail to qualify as a 'price revolution' to modern economists, the fact is they were sustained for almost a century and a half, and both succeeded and preceded long periods of stable or falling prices. Moreover, the rise in prices of consumables outstripped wage-rates by a factor of two to one. This was because with a growing population the supply of labour was greater than the demand. So real wages for agricultural and industrial labour actually fell by up to 50 per cent in the period.

This made it extremely hard for the able-bodied poor to exist, never mind settle down, have families, and aspire to upward social mobility. It also surely contributed to the 'idleness' of which contemporaries endlessly complained, for workers were inclined to choose unemployment instead of the lengthy hours of labour needed to keep pace with price rises. Finally, improvements in productivity were limited. There was no 'industrial revolution', and agricultural production barely kept up with demand.

One way out of the poverty-trap was work in a position of direct dependency. Two-fifths of the labour-force in seventeenth-century villages lived and worked in the households of masters, mostly as servants or in husbandry. In towns the proportion was even higher, at between a half and two-thirds, including apprentices and domestics. The system was common partly because the labour laws required the able-bodied poor to have masters, and those entering established trades to serve seven-year apprenticeships. But it was also popular because it safeguarded young workers against rising prices, since they received board, lodgings, and clothing from masters, as well as a token wage. Even to the comparatively élite apprentices this protection from market-forces must have held some attractions. Governments indeed eventually adopted dependency as a means of relieving the poor and employing vagrants. Yet the system was unstable and led to vagrancy. Servants and masters alike broke contracts, quarrelled, beat one another, and neglected their respective duties. Female servants were made pregnant by male members of households, and were then dismissed. Menials stole from masters and tended to leave them after a year (apprentices excepted). Far from being harmonious, patriarchal households were riven with conflicts.

Another way out of poverty was migration, which probably increased in frequency and distance among the poor (4). Leaving one's native village or town was common, running as high as 15 per cent of the population a year in the 1520s, and at a third per decade in seventeenth-century villages. But among the propertyless it was still higher: persons taxed on wages in the 1520s were seven times more mobile than those assessed on lands and goods. Deaths no doubt accounted for some disappearances, but migration for many others. Young and dependent workers were extraordinarily mobile. First they left their parents to work in better-off homes: in one Middlesex village in 1599 between two-thirds and three-quarters of teenagers and young adults were living in non-parental households. They also moved to other villages and beyond to towns to take up positions. Even then they did not stay put. A half to two-thirds of farm servants changed masters yearly; domestics who stayed longer than a year with a master were exceptional; and most apprentices left town again once their terms finished. Finally, the American colonies took perhaps 200,000 British immigrants in the seventeenth century, many of them poor.

Another mobile group were small-holders, who were forced out of, if not evicted from, common-field villages undergoing agrarian changes. These are usually described as 'enclosures', but the process was more complicated than just erecting hedges. In reality the small-holder was besieged on many fronts. Enclosure involved the change to individual farming from a communal system in open-fields. The result was the extinction of common rights, especially over grazing, upon which small-holders relied heavily. The enclosure process did not cease around 1520, as is sometimes assumed, and indeed continued to 1600 and later.

Engrossing, one wave of which did end about 1520, was another menace to the small man. It involved the absorption of entire farms into larger units, usually for sheep farming. Engrossers wiped out a large share of the 2,000 villages deserted between 1086 and 1700, particularly in the Midlands. Besides enclosure and engrossing, big landholders had other weapons to deploy against small-holders. A good half of manorial tenants had no rights of renewal of their holdings, and two-thirds were liable to increased rents. These were supposed to be 'reasonable', but actually outstripped the rise in food prices. If a tenant could not renew his holding, he would have to move on. When tenure was secure but produced an uneconomic return, lords transferred maintenance responsibilities to tenants, allowed buildings to fall into disrepair, imposed new services, and revived old ones. All told, large landowners were well placed to shift small ones, even though we lack statistics for how many went.

9

Where did the displaced go, and how did they live? The standard response to the first question is 'to the towns', and there is some truth in it. The urban population roughly quadrupled between 1500 and 1700, thus surpassing the general increase in population and producing real urban growth. London was the outstanding case, rising from a town of about 50,000 souls in 1500 to become Europe's largest city in 1700, a metropolis of 575,000. But urban growth was pretty general around the country, even including small towns. Some of the latter grew by a rise in the birth-rate, but in larger towns deaths usually outstripped births, so that these grew by immigration. In London's case 5,700 immigrants must have come in each year between 1604 and 1660 for the place to mushroom at the rate it did. They settled above all in burgeoning suburbs.

The poor were also attracted to forest regions. Woodland villages in the Midlands, for example, grew by 30 to 50 per cent more than open-field ones in the sixteenth and seventeenth centuries, largely because of immigration. In both the suburbs and forests official restraints upon immigration were weak compared to town centres and traditional, nucleated villages. In the outskirts of towns newcomers found cheap accommodation where they escaped the notice of hard-pressed officials. In woodland areas they set up lean-to's and shacks, stole fuel almost at will, and carved out fields and grazing land from the forest. In both suburbs and woodland regions, moreover, they avoided the guild and apprenticeship systems and set up in a multitude of trades. Finally, forest areas offered industrial opportunities such as mining and metallurgy, as well as the ubiquitous cloth industry. By 1600 the fringes in town and country were buzzing with people and production.

But the hopes of migrants were often dashed. Positions as servants and apprentices sheltered them from some price rises, but whether by 1600 many had the capital to set up in a trade or on the land is doubtful. Indeed there are many signs of failures to establish secure moorings by this time, including a rising share of former dependent workers among vagrants. What is more, by 1600 many forests and suburbs were crammed with paupers. Woodland villages in the Midlands had on average 10 to 15 per cent more poor than open-field ones by the 1670s, and the problem was apparent long before that. From the 1580s in London and elsewhere, the suburbs were on the point of being overwhelmed with the hordes of displaced indigents. In both town and country officials began to drive them out by using settlement by-laws. Under the early Stuarts Whitehall even attempted to check immigration by restricting building in London, and to rid woodland areas of squatters by reviving the forest laws. The crown's aims in both instances were blatantly fiscal, but the offences were none the less there to be prosecuted. In the forest regions, officials were rebuffed by riots involving thousands. Vagrants in fact came overwhelmingly from suburbs and woodland areas, a result partly of official clear-outs, but mainly because of the high degree of distress in such places.

Migrants failed to keep footholds for many reasons. The problem was partly sheer numbers. Too many turned up in relation to the available resources and employment chances. But the economic problems of their new homes were also to blame. Pastoral farming was expanded so far in forest areas that eventually, like towns, they had to rely upon outside corn supplies. Moreover, as land ran out they turned to industrial by-employments. This made them 'urban villagers' and, like urban workers, terribly vulnerable. When harvests were poor – roughly once every four years – they were likely to be short of food *and* unemployed. This was because the demand for industrial goods slackened when food prices were high: people could do without new clothing in hard times, but not food. In addition, in the larger towns high mortality rates meant even shorter working-lives than in the country. At the same time, high immigration flooded the labour market with young, inexperienced workers. They laboured in unstable positions of dependency, as we know, but also in the cloth industry, which was subject to collapses and went into quasi-permanent depression after 1614. Finally, even those who escaped to the Americas were not automatically better off there, as we shall see below. In sum, there were few rags-to-riches stories in sixteenth- and early seventeenth-century England.

A final source of poverty and vagrancy was warfare. Tudor and

11

early Stuart armies were not much larger than late medieval ones, but they were still disruptive. This was chiefly because of the new social character of troops. Governments had conscripted vagabonds since Edward III's reign, but from about 1560 armies ceased to be mainly feudal levies and were drawn, at least for overseas campaigns, from the poor and criminal classes. When they returned home, they proved difficult to reintegrate into civilian life. In addition to being poor, they had possibly learned new vices, including expertise with weapons. Moreover, they had no loyalty to the state, whereas the feudal hosts had at least been faithful to their lords. A riot of 500 demobilized men in Westminster in 1589 so terrified the government that it declared martial law and hanged a number of them. Then from 1593 Parliament passed legislation to relieve and employ veterans, which began to have some effect in the early seventeenth century. But during the civil wars of the mid-seventeenth century the system was overwhelmed by the demand for assistance. The problem did not stop with the troops themselves. The system of 'impressment' or conscription hit the poor hardest, for the wealthy bought their sons out, as Shakespeare's Falstaff found to his profit in *Henry IV, Part One*. Most recruits were probably young and unmarried, but families left by the minority who were breadwinners could be plunged into poverty by their departures.

The side-effects of sustained warfare first posed major threats in the Twenty Years War against Spain from 1585 to 1604, when upwards of 80,000 men fought in the different campaigns. The problem recurred under James I and Charles I when major forces were raised in the 1620s and 1630s, first to fight in the Thirty Years War, and then against the Scots. Besides those demobbed, there were further difficulties with troops. Deserters were rife, sometimes as many as a third to a half of forces, and they had to be rounded up. Moreover, armies were usually recruited *ad hoc*, since, unlike continental states, England had no permanent or standing army. Such hurried attempts at making war resulted in mismanagement and disastrous campaigns, like the Earl of Leicester's in the Low Countries in 1585 and the Duke of Buckingham's in France in 1627. No wonder then that military men were more and more common among vagrants from the late sixteenth century. Of course disbanded armies caused social problems before 1560, as Thomas More's *Utopia* of 1516 shows. When forces no longer comprised loyal tenants of some substance, but ragged and poorly organized conscripts, then the problem became even more serious.

Tudor and early Stuart England thus faced a massive poverty problem which posed a real threat to public order. Although the poor appear largely to have lacked class consciousness, governments faced a number of popular rebellions in which the poor participated and in which egalitarian ideas surfaced. Learned and official opinion was under no illusions that poverty and vagrancy were real menaces. Possibly a good half of the population were unable to support themselves at the beginning of the period, and matters worsened until at least 1650. In reality, there was no solution to the Tudor and early Stuart poverty problem, short of a social revolution (always a remote possibility) in which wealth and power were radically redistributed. Just the same, officials intervened precisely to ensure that that did not happen.

The response

PERCEPTIONS OF POVERTY | ATTITUDES

In this society a tiny minority, at most a few thousand men, ran things, forming opinion as well as policy. To understand the latter one must examine the former, for policies were not attempts willy-nilly to deal with a worsening problem, nor the result of state-building for its own sake. The principles of the poor-laws were clear and remarkably consistent over a century and more: to punish the 'wilfully idle' and to relieve the disabled. Their development over the period is also evident. Governments were generally hostile to the vagabond and created numerous institutions to deal with him. Only from about 1650 did attitudes soften and the emphasis upon punishment diminish. The rule throughout was to relieve the disabled, at first by voluntary means, but later by means of a statutory tax. Towns often took the lead in developing these policies, but by the mid-seventeenth century they were widely enforced in the countryside as well.

13

Hand-outs to beggars came under attack in the sixteenth century, especially when given to 'sturdy' ones. From monarch to parish priest, those in power pilloried the idle and vagabond. Henry VIII himself amended a statement in the *Bishop's Book* of 1537 that the rich should succour the poor, to exclude those who 'live by the graft of begging slothfully'. A century later the rector of Wenden Lofts in Essex declared that beggars were generally 'dissolute, disobedient, and reprobate to every good work'. Along with witches, they were the real bogey-men of the time.

The explanation of this attitude, historians have concluded, lies in a distinct Protestant position on wealth and poverty. Basically, the argument is that Protestants, uncertain of their salvation, experienced anxiety that drove them into worldly activity as a way of finding confirmation of their 'election'. Thus, despite Protestantism's rejection of 'good works' as a way to Heaven, they found solace from similar sources. But instead of charitable work, it was work *per se* that brought consolation. Labouring in one's calling, diligence, thrift and success were seen as signs of salvation. Conversely, the wilfully idle were clearly damned. The Puritan William Perkins attacked them as 'the very seminary of vagabonds, rogues, and straggling persons, which have no calling'. Indeed they were 'thieves and robbers, because they steal their labour from the church and commonwealth'. Other Protestants castigated them as 'drone bees, that live upon the spoil of the poor bees'; that is, they took relief from the genuinely needy. When Puritans were actually in power in the 1640s and 1650s, it is sometimes alleged, they took a hard line towards the poor, even stopping relief. In recent years Professor Jordan has taken this old view of the 'Protestant ethic' regarding poverty and stood it on its head. He suggests that English Protestants were in fact extraordinarily generous to the poor, at least the worthy ones. They endowed charities for them rather than handing out casual alms as medieval Catholics had done. They also assisted them by giving more to secular than to religious causes (12).

There are serious difficulties with this explanation of poor-relief. One is that neither Protestant nor Puritan treatment of the poor has been shown to be different from the Roman Catholics'. The case for a distinct Protestant or Puritan position remains

14

therefore unproven. In the meantime, the signs are that the decision could go the other way. Thus medieval canon lawyers were critical of idleness chosen for sinful reasons. Moreover, the first sixteenth-century religious writers to call for the suppression of begging and the relief of the disabled were Catholics: John Major, a Scottish theologian teaching at the Sorbonne in Paris, and Thomas More, both in 1516. Then numerous Catholic states, like Protestant ones, sought in subsequent decades to put ideas like these into effect. Nor had Protestants a monopoly on endowed charities with secular aims. Catholic states like Venice possessed a number of such foundations both in the pre- and post-Reformation periods; typically religious bequests like masses for the dead declined in Catholic Lyons from the late fifteenth century while those for the poor rose; and in pre-Reformation London charity was not wholly religious, and the only differences with giving after 1540 were in degree rather than kind (21).

Furthermore, Protestant and Puritan positions regarding the poor were more complex than is usually supposed. Begging, for instance, was not wholly outlawed in the English legislation. In fact, governments actually licensed large numbers of beggars. Even the sharpest Puritan critics of mendicancy, for that matter, shrank from complete refusals of alms out of fear of endangering their souls. It is also incorrect to assume that Protestants always gave charity with secular aims in mind. The Calvinist anxious about his salvation could slip into positions that came very close to the Catholic doctrine of good works. The Puritan John Downame wrote in 1616 that by giving charity 'we make our calling and election sure' and that 'by these works of mercy we are furthered notably in the way to salvation'. Equally dubious is the line that after 1540 the dole to the poor at funerals, which Jordan considered a 'typical, but on the whole wasteful, if not harmful, form of medieval almsgiving', was 'superseded by endowments most carefully established and regulated'. But funeral doles did not die out under Protestantism. Dole-type gifts generally remained the most common at roughly 80 per cent of the total, with endowments far behind at about 10 per cent, in Elizabethan and early Stuart Warwick. 'Medieval' habits of giving therefore persisted until the time of Oliver Cromwell and in some places longer. Finally, when the work of Puritan magistrates of the 1640s and 1650s is examined locally, far from being severe towards the poor, they turn out to have been exceptionally active in relieving them. In Warwickshire the bench issued almost three times as many orders for relief from 1649 to 1660 as the justices from 1630 to 1641 (3).

If Protestantism was not crucial in forming early-modern attitudes towards the poor, what other forces were at work? Certainly one common spur to attacking the poverty problem was political. Governments in many places were extending their authority in an age well known for the 'rise of the modern state'. But there was more to the poor-laws than state-building as an end in itself. To governments all over western Europe, small and large, Catholic and Protestant, poverty posed a threat. Beggars and vagrants were feared for fomenting sedition and rebellion, spreading disease, and all manner of disorder, even witchcraft. A proclamation of 1497 actually blamed them for 'heinous murders, robberies, thefts, decay of husbandry, and other enormities and inconveniences'. It was reasoned that if the sedentary poor were not relieved, they would soon turn into rogues. Considering the size and vulnerability of the propertyless class, this was sound thinking.

The call for state action was developed in three quite distinct lines of thought. One was the 'literature of roguery', a sizeable body of popular tracts that purported to expose the misdeeds of an underworld of beggars and tramps. It described their habits and haunts, specialized techniques for theft, fraudulent methods of begging, gang organizations, and secret jargon. The literature appeared in all the major western European languages. Even though many of its tales were far-fetched, its implicit message reinforced official fears: that the dispossessed were disorderly and criminal and, if left to their own devices, would overthrow those in power. We know the literature was popular because examples were translated, republished in further editions, and even pirated. Some writers wrote them for a living. The tracts were also influential. Gentlemen's libraries contained examples, even ones in foreign languages, and the learned gave them credence. Whether the 'underworld' was as extensive and dangerous as the

16

authors claimed is doubtful, but their readers undoubtedly believed it was.

A second influential line on poverty was the work of so-called 'commonwealth' thinkers. The basic assumption here, which dated from the Middle Ages, was that society was an organism whose inter-dependent parts worked together so that the 'body commonwealth' could function. The monarch was often portrayed as the head or the heart, magistrates as the eyes, artisans as the hands, and husbandmen as the feet. This view had two applications to the poverty issue. First, in a living body no parts could be idle because then it would cease to function properly. Second, since society comprised mutually dependent parts, the rich were supposed to look after the poor in their needs, while the latter had the obligation to serve the former and labour faithfully in their callings. This organic theory of society enjoyed a great vogue among the learned and powerful of the sixteenth century. Its great appeal was that it mended an increasingly tattered social fabric.

The third important influence upon policy was Renaissance humanism. By humanism we do not mean modern humanitarianism, nor a philosophy concerned with matters human as opposed to divine. Rather the term refers to the course of study followed by the Renaissance humanist with its emphasis upon classical learning. But it is not the particulars of humanistic studies that relate to the poverty issue; rather their implicit message and application. The humanists' studies were founded upon the belief that people could be improved, morally and intellectually, through the study of the classics. This principle in theory respected no barriers of class or sex: the poor might be educated and even rise to positions of authority; so might women. Indeed, that political power should be based upon merit, not birth, was a precept among English humanists of the 1530s. Although in reality most humanists concerned themselves with the education of the élites, the implication of their stand on education was that poverty was not inevitable. Through education, at least in a trade, the fit poor could be reformed and found work. Delinquent children might be taken off the streets and educated in schools; even prostitutes might be 'corrected' to lead honest lives. Indeed all these crimes might be checked if idleness were stopped, for it was the root of these evils. So a condemnation of beggary and vagabondage followed naturally from the humanists' belief in moral improvement through education.

It also followed from their favouring of an active as opposed to a contemplative life. Humanists generally viewed worldly activity as a good thing and saw no value in idleness. Indeed they utterly condemned those who chose it, including monks as well as beggars. Thus, contrary to the Franciscan ideal of poverty, so powerful in the High Middle Ages, that the poor were holy and the holy should be poor, the humanists saw dangers in material deprivation. It led to temptation, to sin and to crime. But if one were rich, one was less subject to such traps and might actually help remedy poverty through charitable works.

These ideas might have remained purely theoretical had humanists not been interested in politics. Their commitment to political action of course arose from their interest in worldly activity. In their opinion the educated had more than the right to involve themselves in government; they had the duty. From the late fourteenth century humanists were active in Italian politics. The same tendency appeared in England under Henry VII and Henry VIII. The latter chose Thomas More as his chancellor and employed a number of lesser humanist lights as propagandists and tutors. In line with their belief in political activity, humanists proposed solutions for the poverty problem. Thomas More's *Utopia* took the vagrancy issue as its starting-point for an analysis of England's social ills in 1516; Juan-Luis Vives, a Spanish humanist with close English links, wrote the most influential tract on poverty of the period, *On the Relief of the Poor*, in 1526; and Thomas Cromwell's circle in the 1530s, which included the humanists Richard Morison and Thomas Starkey, produced plans to employ vagabonds and relieve the disabled.

So the humanists' attack upon idleness came from a number of directions. They believed that the slothful could be reformed because they believed in education; that they should be dealt with because an active life was preferable to an idle one; and that, with humanist assistance, plans could be devised to reform the poor. Their critique of poverty was perhaps the single most important

18

influence upon policy-makers in early modern Europe. In addition to their personal involvement in government, their doctrines became established in schools and universities in Catholic and Protestant lands alike.

UNOFFICIAL CHARITY

It remains to examine the responses to poverty after 1500. It might seem strange that governments should abolish facilities for poor-relief at a time when the demand was growing, but this is what happened in England between 1536 and 1549. First, from 1536 to 1539 over 800 monastic houses were dissolved. Then from 1545 to 1549, 500 hospitals and an undetermined number of almshouses and religious guilds were wound up in the so-called 'Chantries' Acts. The motives and many consequences of this 'great transfer', the greatest shift in land ownership since the Conquest, will not bear retelling here, but the effects upon poor-relief are germane. These have long been the subject of debate, often from Catholic or Protestant positions, but since the work of the Russian Alexander Savine early in this century the picture has become less muddied. He showed that on average perhaps as little as 2.5 per cent of monastic income went on charity to the poor (16). But he warned that his main source, the *Valor Ecclesiasticus* of church wealth of 1535, 'does not give a complete idea of monastic charity' because only compulsory gifts were recorded. In addition, there were casual alms, leftovers from the monks' tables, hospitality to passers-by, the beneficence of abbots and their almoners. Dom David Knowles reckons that such casual giving could double or treble the proportion of income devoted to charity, which then might have been as high as 10 per cent (12).

It is difficult to weigh up the results of the loss of monastic relief. Certainly the dissolutions hit certain towns quite hard, including Abingdon, Bury St Edmunds, Coventry, Oxford, Peterborough and Warwick. But rarely are we able to observe the effects on the poor themselves. It is possible, through, to compare the monks' charity with statutory relief in the seventeenth century. Such calculations involve much guesswork, but suggest that if monastic relief had been paid out at the same rate as in 1535,

Table 1 Monastic Charity and State Poor-Relief Compared

	Estimated Relief
Monastic Charity* 1535	£11,500
Monastic Charity 1614 (notional value)†	£76,500
Monastic Charity 1650 (notional value)†	£94,500
State Relief 1614	£30,000–£40,000
State Relief 1650	£188,000–£250,000

* Based on median figures for income (£180,000) and expenditure on charity (6.25%).

† Assuming that prices had risen 3.4 times by 1611–20 and 4.2 times by 1641–50 (over 1531–40); that population and numbers of the poor had doubled (14).

it might have been twice as high as statutory payments in 1614 and as much as 50 per cent of the mid-seventeenth century total (see Table 1). Of course one obvious objection is that we do not know how effective the monks' money was in relieving poverty. It is possible that parish payments were more carefully administered than monastic ones, particularly in distinguishing the slothful from the genuinely needy. But in reality we do not know enough about the mechanics of either to say. Whatever the case, the figures do not suggest that monastic charity was insignificant.

There is no doubt, moreover, that the dissolution of the monasteries involved a substantial over-all sum. If, for instance, instead of selling the lands off, the crown had applied a major share of monastic revenue, say a quarter, to poor-relief, the total would have surpassed indoor and outdoor relief as late as 1696. A quarter of the monks' revenues were worth £387,000 by that time, inflation and population taken into account, compared with an estimated £350,000 spent on relief then. Instead, the crown completely wasted the church lands, selling them off over the following decades, and using the proceeds to fight wars. Yet employing them for social purposes was not a utopian proposition at the time. Even arch-enemies of the monks like Dr John London, politicians like Audley and Wriothesley who profited from the dissolutions, and zealous Protestants like Latimer sought to save part of the windfall for relieving and employing the poor.

By contrast, German Protestant states took far greater care to ensure that church properties were kept for charitable and educational ends. In England it was mainly the already rich who gained.

The hospitals, almshouses, and guilds dissolved in Edward vi's reign also require fresh examination. The first numbered about 500 foundations, and although many had small incomes and were badly run they still obviously provided some succour. A number survived the Chantries Acts, but others were sold off, and we remain in the dark as to the final balance. Religious guilds are even more obscure in regard both to numbers and survival. All that can definitely be said about them and the other foundations is that their dissolutions represent a further unquantifiable loss of relief. But the fact that some new owners continued foundations after dissolution (as required by the Suppression Act of 1536) does not mean that assistance kept pace with inflation or the demand. Clearly the dissolutions cannot be said to have 'caused' early-modern poverty. On the other hand, to abolish institutions with the capability of relieving it was disastrous.

A final issue of the dissolutions that might have contributed to vagrancy was the fate of the 9,000 or so servants of the houses. Their lot was probably much less kind than that of the monks and nuns, most of whom received pensions or secured new positions. The new owners of the lands were supposed to maintain 'hospitality' according to statute and keep on former employees, but the lack of evidence of enforcement makes one suspicious. In fact we do not know what happened to ex-servants. Certainly, if a very large share were not retained, this would have swollen the ranks of vagabonds.

According to Professor Jordan's findings, post-Reformation charity made up whatever losses resulted from the dissolutions. From a multi-volume study of ten countries he concluded that bequests for poor-relief increased ten-fold from 1540 to 1660. But a number of criticisms have been levelled at this study. Attention has mainly focused upon the failure to take price inflation into account. When this is done, the result is a largely stagnant curve instead of a dramatic rise, since consumables' prices rose about six-fold in the period. More recent writing, though, suggests that 'deflating' the figures is not enough. In addition one must calculate the ongoing yields of charities. After all, simply to reckon up the original value of a bequest takes no account of the benefits it continued to yield in later decades, even centuries. When the continuing revenues are thus calculated, the picture looks different from the 'deflated' one. Even allowing for price rises and a doubling of the need because of population growth, total charity rose roughly four times over from 1540 to 1660 and produced a *per capita* increase in poor relief, it is argued (8).

There still exist major problems with recent studies of charity. One concerns the evidence, mainly derived from people's wills. These do not record all giving, for casual hand-outs continued and are imperfectly documented. What is more, gifts were sometimes left in kind, and how does one quantify a university education or succour to a man in prison? Moreover, we cannot assume that, once established, charities were actually administered. The records of many, perhaps most, foundations are scrappy for most of the period. When specific cases are studied, some turn out to have had lapses in administration, to have been of limited benefit to the places where they were located, or occasionally never to have got off the ground. Large donations are also hard to interpret. Henry VII and two early Stuart London merchants left huge sums to the poor, which account for large proportions of the total giving in their respective periods. These gifts are registered as steep rises on graphs of charity. Yet should two or three bequests be considered signs of great increases in giving by the population at large? Probably not.

A final point concerns comparisons with amounts raised by poor-rates. Thus Jordan collected evidence of public relief and concluded that the £20,000 to £30,000 raised from rates in 1651–60 was far less than charitable bequests, which he reckoned at over £100,000 in that decade. But this interpretation makes no allowance for lost records. There are undoubtedly many parishes whose documents have not survived. But where records are good, public relief dwarfed the yields of charities. In seventeenth-century Shropshire poor-rates produced five to ten times the amounts coming from bequests, and in London between 1640 and 1660 the picture was similar (9). At the end of the day it seems that

22

accurate figures for charitable giving, whether pre- or post-Reformation, will elude the historian. This is mainly because he lacks evidence of the administration of both, apart from local cases. The losses of the dissolutions were undoubtedly great, and potential sources to relieve social problems were wasted. Charity still continued to flow from private hands after 1540, but its impact is uncertain. Certainly it did not remove the need for statutory relief.

STATE POOR-RELIEF

The poor-laws included provision both for the relief of the disabled and for the chastisement of the fit. Few statutes dealt uniquely with one of the two groups, and in practice attempts to discriminate between them broke down. Some of the able-bodied in actuality received relief, and the disabled were sometimes punished. Yet the division into two separate policies is useful for purposes of analysis.

The sixteenth century saw slow but steady progress towards statutory poor-relief. The right of the disabled poor to assistance had been regulated in fourteenth-century labour-laws, but they only implied the right by denying it to the able-bodied. Even as late as 1495 and 1531 Acts of Parliament mainly aimed to keep the poor from wandering (see Appendix for details of these and other statutes). A major change came in new legislation in 1536, when we see the germ of a state, parish-based relief system. The Act ordered churchwardens 'or two others' weekly to gather alms, which were to be distributed via 'common boxes and common gatherings'. As before, casual doles were discouraged. The statute thus made a significant leap forward in naming officials responsible for relief. The 'slavery' Act of 1547, despite its infamous reputation, took things a stage further. First, it ordered local officials to provide housing for all 'idle, impotent, maimed, and aged persons' who were not vagabonds; second, it provided that weekly collections be gathered in the parish church for their succour. Another Edwardian statute of 1552 was the first to introduce an element of compulsion in poor-relief. Anyone who refused to contribute was to be 'exhorted' by the parson, and if he persisted in back-sliding, to be referred to the bishop. Already by the mid-sixteenth century, therefore, some major principles of relief under the poor-laws were emerging: each parish's responsibility for its own disabled; parish administration, supervised by higher officials; and regular collections to which all (financially) able householders were to contribute.

The Elizabethan poor-relief legislation is notable mainly for building on the principle of compulsory giving, which by the end of the reign was indeed the law of the land. And when enforced, as it gradually was, it wrought a revolution in government with far-reaching effects. An Act of 1563 went far beyond that of 1552 in this direction. It stated that anyone refusing to contribute to collections could be bound to appear before justices, and if they continued to demur, to be imprisoned. The law also laid down penalties for officials who did not gather collections. Here evidently was a serious attempt to develop the rule of compulsory relief regarding those supposed to give and to collect alms. By comparison, further Acts of 1572 and 1576 added little regarding the disabled poor.

Later Acts of 1597 and 1601 are often considered the crowning achievements of the Elizabethan poor-relief legislation. So they were in the sense that little new followed them, but in reality they were more important in codifying existing principles than in creating new ones. The first statute formally named overseers of the poor as the chief parochial officers in charge of collections and relief, and ordered them to be appointed in all parishes. It also made provisions for compelling any persons refusing to pay what was a poor-tax in all but name. Otherwise the laws of 1597 and 1601 mainly dotted the 'i's' and crossed the 't's'; the latter in fact largely re-enacted the former. The first Act provided that housing be built at parish expense on waste or common land, with the agreement of the lord of the manor. As before, begging was limited; in this instance to one's home parish, only for 'relief of victuals', and with the consent of the overseers and church-wardens. The law also stipulated that neighbouring parishes share relief costs if one was more heavily burdened with poor, which was also suggested in previous Acts. But even if the chief provisions of the late Elizabethan laws on relief were not wholly novel, these Acts were re-enacted and remained the foundation-stones of the system under the Stuarts.

In addition to relieving the disabled, the legislation sought to employ the able poor. Sometimes work was prescribed as a remedy for begging, as in 1531 and 1536, and occasionally as a means of putting the poor generally to work. Thus in 1536 children aged from 5 to 14 could be placed in service in husbandry, and later Acts of 1547, 1549 and 1572 contained similar provisions. Then in 1576 was passed 'an Act for the setting of the poor on work', which made more detailed orders. All corporate towns were to raise stocks of wool and other materials, and to build 'houses of correction'. In them the young, as well as rogues and vagabonds, would be put to labour, and to support them county-wide rates were to be levied. Later, in statutes of 1597 and 1610, the children of the poor were again to be 'apprenticed'. But parliament was not the sole source of plans to create work for the poor. Nor had Protestants a monopoly on the 'work-ethic'. Projects in fact crop up throughout the period in various guises: in More's *Utopia* as early as 1516; in a poor-law draft of 1536; in privately initiated schemes for developing everything from cloth manufacture to fishing fleets and overseas colonies; and in the London Corporation of the Poor and other proposals in the 1640s and 1650s.

Another area of poor-relief activity outside Parliament was the town. Indeed many towns anticipated statutes with their own independent initiatives. They even created special institutions such as London's Bridewell, a former royal palace converted to a work-house in 1553, which was probably the model for statutory houses of correction. Urban centres had numerous problems that made them likely candidates for early action on poor-law matters. Many were suffering from London's competition for trade and had depressed economies up to 1600. Yet they were also centres of immigration and population growth, if not at the same rate as the capital. The Edwardian dissolutions of hospitals and almshouses, moreover, forced their hands, for these institutions were generally located in towns. Finally, towns were centres of intellectual and religious activity. So when reformers like Thomas More and Hugh Latimer attempted to make England a more Christian society by relieving the poor, urban places were natural laboratories. Even a small town like Warwick found its apostle in the 1580s: Thomas Cartwright, perhaps the leading Puritan of the period, and master of the Earl of Leicester's hospital there in 1587. He organized a census of the town's poor that year, and personally decided who should receive relief.

The towns pioneered a number of novel poor-relief measures, one of which was indeed the census. The earliest is that for Norwich in 1570 in which the names, ages and trades of all the English poor of the city were listed by household and parish. The thoroughness of such surveys can be seen in examples from Warwick, St Mary's, in 1587:

> Roger Bredon of age 50 years, has a wife 50 years [old], and a child named Elizabeth. The mother and daughter beg.

> Miles Atown of the age of 60 years, has Isabel his wife aged 48 years; have four children, viz. Thomas, 10 years, William, 7 years, William the younger, 4 years, and Alice [a] half year old. They all beg.

> Elizabeth wife of John Nichols, fugitive. She is of age 70 years. She is almost blind, was born in the town, and is lame.

The authorities sought such detailed information to determine people's conditions in order to 'means-test' them; that is, to decide whether they needed or merited assistance, and if so, how much. If they were young and able to work, officials might decide to apprentice them. If they were old, disabled, or burdened with many children, they might be considered worthy of relief. If, on the other hand, they were immigrants who had lived there a short time, they might be refused relief and even sent away to their previous dwelling places. Finally, if they had trades but were unemployed, they might be set to labouring in a bridewell. But fundamentally the census was a means of limiting those receiving relief. Thus in Warwick in 1587, of 245 persons listed in the Cartwright survey, 22 were immediately despatched from the town because they were recent arrivals. Of the remaining 223, possibly just 127, or just over half, were relieved with poor-rates. Likewise in St Martin's parish, Salisbury, in 1635, a third of the population were listed as poor, but only 4 per cent were allotted aid.

Another method developed to limit poor-relief was to require the poor to wear badges. Then only those wearing the proper insignia were relieved. It is uncertain how the practice originated. Possibly it derived from the regulation in the Middle Ages of those other 'deviants', the Jews, who were made to don yellow crosses. Whatever the case, it became common in Renaissance Europe. Officials in Tudor towns used the device, and in Elizabethan and later Stuart poor-laws it was actually extended to the whole country.

Towns also assisted the poor with corn supplies. The policy of the traditional 'open' market in towns was that prices should be controlled and 'just', that all dealings should be public, and that the poor should be specially provisioned in times of shortage. Clashing with this custom was the reality of increasing private dealing by middlemen for maximum profit, in which the interests of the poor received short shrift. So governments intervened to regulate trade. Whitehall issued proclamations on average every other year from 1485 to 1603, and ordered searches for corn supplies in 'Books of Orders' in 1587, 1608, 1621–3 and 1629–31. The aims were to stop hoarding and to see that the poor were supplied, especially in years of scarcity. Finally, Parliament passed legislation to control exports and middlemen. In addition to central directives, towns took initiatives, in times of poor harvests importing corn and storing it. Officials also clamped down on brewing, which consumed vast amounts of barley that in a pinch could be made into bread. In one remarkable instance, that of Salisbury in 1625, the authorities actually took over the industry and ran a 'common brewhouse'. Thus they killed two birds with one stone, for in addition to regulating brewing, they employed the poor in the house (17).

Towns also devised other schemes to employ those in distress. These institutions were not exclusively penal, at least in intent. Numerous towns had plans to set the 'honest poor' to work, especially in the cloth industry. Before houses of correction were the law of the land in 1576, Lincoln, London and Norwich had taken such action. The possibility was considered even in a small place like Warwick in 1571, when the Earl of Leicester encouraged the city fathers to establish a 'special trade' like cloth- or cap-making. He hoped it would keep large numbers busy: 'workmen and -women and such may therein be employed as in no faculty else.' Even children could spin and card wool, while the lame might pick and fray it. In Norwich, Salisbury and Wakefield work-schemes were running for some years; but whether they had much long-term impact on unemployment is doubtful.

Finally, towns levied poor-rates. Some had already raised funds in this way in the fifteenth century, but still more did so in the sixteenth. No doubt in part they were influenced by the increased statutory responsibility laid on localities by parliament. But even before compulsory rates came in, some municipalities levied them: London in 1547, Cambridge in 1556, Ipswich in 1557, and many others thereafter. Professor Jordan indeed unearthed evidence of close to 200 rates in towns in the decade from 1601 to 1610 alone. Taxing for poor-relief was not always a straightforward matter, however. In the case of Warwick legal battles resulted, lasting over seven years and reflecting deep divisions in the corporation.

Despite the early steps by towns to relieve the poor, it would be misleading to think that country areas lagged far behind. In part the impression of urban precociousness is an illusion created by better record-keeping. Nevertheless, evidence of poor-relief exists for rural areas before 1640. As in towns, we find censuses of the poor, as well as efforts to ensure they were victualled in times of scarcity. Nor were rural parishes all that much slower off the mark in levying poor-rates. There is evidence of levies in Essex as early as 1555, or less than a decade after London first taxed its citizens. William Harrison claimed in 1577 that poor-relief was already an established fact, stating that 'there is order taken throughout every parish in the realm that weekly collection[s] shall be made for their help and sustentation'. Then in 1579 the Queen's physician estimated that relief was 'a greater tax than some subsidies', a 'larger collection than would maintain yearly a good army', which must have been several thousand pounds.

We begin to find confirmation of these sweeping statements from the 1580s. In Wiltshire a number of persons were fined for not paying rates and for refusing to be collectors. Then after the

Act of 1597 made rates statutory there are signs of widespread enforcement in country areas. In two areas of Warwickshire in 1605 only 11 of 100 parishes were reported to be delinquent in administration. The government gave a major boost to the system in the 1630s with the policy of 'Thorough'. A 'Book of Orders' was issued to local justices that included provisions for the relief of the poor. But the policy of Charles I's government contained no new principles and was motivated by the fear of disorder as much as by 'state paternalism'. Indeed once central direction ceased in the turmoil of civil war from 1642, JPs still kept the system going in line with Tudor principles. So by 1650 statutory rates and relief were established institutions. By 1660 Jordan found that three-quarters of the surviving records of poor-rates came from rural parishes, and we know that statutory levies were far outstripping relief from private bequests by this time. The conclusion is inescapable that poor-relief was widely enforced in mid-seventeenth-century England.

Assistance was mainly in the form of weekly cash doles, but housing, medical care, clothing, fuel, apprenticeships, some primary education, and burial expenses were also provided. The able-bodied as well as the 'impotent' were in fact relieved. What is more, the system was responsive to crises like harvest failures and trade slumps. In seventeenth-century Hampshire and Warwickshire we have evidence that relief payments were normally increased in response to such disasters. Counties also authorized general collections for the victims of fires, shipwrecks and wars. Whereas in France of the period the poor starved and rioted when food ran short, in England the poor-relief system gave them some protection. By 1650, therefore, this country had a powerful weapon for checking poverty on a national scale, funded by statutory taxes and administered by state officials. In the Europe of 1650 that was no mean achievement and undoubtedly contributed to England's long-term social stability compared with other states.

'MASTERLESS MEN'

We have observed the preconditions of a vagrancy problem in the period: a large and growing landless class; unemployment and underemployment; upward spirals in population, prices and migration; a drop in real wages of up to 50 per cent; and fragile labour-relations between masters and dependent workers. We have also noted how the learned and powerful reacted to unemployment, attacking 'idleness' because they feared the disorders to which it led. It remains to examine the state's response.

The late medieval labour laws first specified who vagrants were in the sense used in the Tudor and Stuart period. Liable to prosecution were all able-bodied persons without independent means, who were unemployed or refused to work for statutory wages. The laws required them to serve for a year at least, and to carry a testimonial or passport when out of service. So for the bondage of villeinage was substituted that of statutory service. We know that compulsory service was enforced in the decades following the Black Death, even if justices were unable to control wages. And even though economic conditions were quite different from 1500 to 1650, the authorities maintained these labour controls because they still saw unemployment as a threat. Indeed they developed a formidable arsenal to combat the problem. Considering the worsening plight of the poor in the period, who would claim that their fears were unfounded?

The statutory definition of vagrancy remained labour-based after 1500. In an Act of 1531 vagabonds included:

> any man or woman whole and mighty in body and able to labour, having no land, master, nor using any lawful merchandise, craft, or mystery whereby he [sic] might get his living.

The formula varied in later statutes, but basically it was the unemployed, fit poor who were at risk. More particularly, and not surprisingly in view of the rising birth-rate, the young were seen as the greatest menace and were specially cited in many Acts. In addition, governments sought to control a great array of 'dangerous trades' through the vagrancy laws: pedlars and tinkers; all types of entertainer, from fiddlers to actors; soldiers and sailors; healers; students and clerics; and wizards. An odd collection, to say the least, but officials required them to carry testimonials like servants, or licensed them. What these diverse

30

jobs had in common was that the authorities perceived them as threats to the *status quo*: hawkers and tinkers because they were exceptionally footloose, literally living on the road; showpeople because they gathered crowds of people together and might cause riots; military men because of their experience of arms and violence; medical practitioners because unlicensed ones violated newly formed monopolies of the physicians and surgeons; clerics and students because they too were mobile and might be political and religious dissidents; and wizards because magic was suspect. Finally, the laws were even deployed to catch petty thieves, prostitutes, drunkards, vandals and persons simply described as 'disorderly'. But above all the statutes were intended to keep the 'sturdy' in service under masters.

Parliament might pass sweeping legislation against idleness, but was it enforced? Local government in this period has been lumbered with a Dogberry image; that is, of the ineffective constable in Shakespeare's *Much Ado About Nothing*. It is true that most officials were part-time, unpaid amateurs who were powerless against major uprisings. But where their interests were substantially in accord with Whitehall's, they could be effective. Certainly in poor-law matters, with the partial exception of compulsory taxation, the parochial élites of town and country had considerable stakes. They feared the disorder and crime that might result from unchecked poverty as much as MPs and ministers; perhaps more so, since they were more directly in the firing line. In fact we have no difficulty finding evidence that the vagrancy laws were enforced. From top to bottom, English government records before 1640 are filled with evidence of attempts to check it. We have continuous records of arrests from a half-dozen Elizabethan and early Stuart towns; and after 1603, for nearly as many counties. Constables' accounts show these much-abused officers regularly ensuring that convicted vagabonds were conveyed 'home', and keeping lists of those they had punished. Finally, when higher officials called upon lesser ones to report evidence of action, local examples suggest 80 per cent at least complied and 50 per cent had actually enforced the law. Of course there were negligent and crooked officials, but even modern governments have these problems.

31

Just how seriously those who ruled took the vagrancy issue is shown by the many institutions employed to deal with it. Governments mounted special round-ups or searches, which had medieval precedents but were first conducted on a national scale under the Tudors and early Stuarts. These included special watches every fortnight, the interrogation of travellers, and arrests of any rogues among them. From 1569 to 1572 we have reports from 18 counties, listing details of more than 750 vagrants seized. Then from 1631 to 1639 there survive records from 37 counties in which over 26,000 were reported apprehended, with details of 5,000 of them (names, places of origin and arrest). The searches involved lengthy chains of command, from the Privy Council through sheriffs and JPs, down to constables. These are impressive results, considering many records have probably disappeared: in less than a decade under Charles I possibly 0.5 per cent of the total population were arrested, or the equivalent of 275,000 persons in Britain today. Both the search campaigns were organized in times when governments were on edge about law and order. But Wiltshire evidence suggests that searches could be sustained for longer periods, as an Act of 1610 specified.

Governments began to use martial law against vagrants in the reign of Henry VIII. Rebels and veterans were the first targets of the 'provost-marshals' appointed then, but they were soon authorized to deal with civilians, including 'idle, vagrant persons, and masterless men'; even fishwives selling without licences in London in 1603. No cases of summary execution of vagrants have been found, although a proclamation of 1616 ordered it. Nevertheless, the marshals were an effective paramilitary force. Deployed in town and country alike, they were often more effective than local officials. They went on horseback, thus covering much more territory than the latter. They were also full-time, well-paid, armed, and went with bands of deputies. As well as arresting rogues, they probably frightened the life out of many. But some jurists had reservations about the legality of the office.

Another new procedure employed against vagrants was summary justice, which again worried jurists. Beginning in 1495 most vagrancy laws granted to constables and justices the authority to try and punish suspects out of court. So the vast majority of convicted vagabonds never saw a jury, unless they were accused of felonies. But to some officials, including MPs, summary trial was a disturbing innovation, for it might violate chapter 39 of Magna Carta, which guaranteed a trial by one's peers to all free men.

A number of punishments were meted out to vagrants, some of them new. Traditional medieval penalties involving redress – the compensation of the victim, or penance – were irrelevant in most vagrancy cases because few offenders had the money to pay fines. In any case, their 'crimes' were not normally against specific persons who could be compensated. Instead their misdeeds arose from their status; that is, their masterless condition. So retributive chastisements were created, including corporal punishment and loss of freedom. Branding, ear-boring, the pillory and hair-cropping all date from late fourteenth-century statutes, but were also used in the sixteenth and seventeenth centuries. The first two were actually administered after new Acts authorized them in 1572 and 1604 respectively. Vagrancy was a felony for repeat offenders in statutes passed in 1536, 1572, 1576, 1597 and 1604, and a few were hanged under the first two Elizabethan Acts. Ear-cropping and the ducking-stool were also punishments for the crime. But all the foregoing penalties were rare compared with flogging, which was a sixteenth-century creation. Whipping was widely employed against all manner of 'inferiors' – pupils, students, children, servants, and apprentices – so it was 'natural' to beat vagrants. It was also a cheap and efficient way of punishment compared with gaols and houses of correction. Moreover, flogging accorded well with the authority summarily to try. Not only did miscreants not have to be held for trial; they could be punished forthwith. These procedures also suited the needs of the local notables administering justice. They gained considerable power from them, which they could utilize efficiently.

Although most commonly corporal, retributive penalties also included various forms of loss of freedom. The Statute of Labourers of 1349 ordered stocks to be set up in every village to punish fugitive labourers. Then an Act of 1495 commanded that vagabonds and beggars be placed in them for three days and nights with a diet of bread and water. Vagabonds were indeed locked up in stocks in the sixteenth century, which were commonly located in market-places and on village greens. Compulsory labour was another statutory punishment. An Act of 1547 placed convicts in slavery for two years, and one of 1597 sent them to serve in galleys, but no evidence has been found that either was enforced. On the other hand, provisions in 1572 that vagrants serve 'honest householders' for one year were put into effect, as were those placing young persons in service and apprenticeships. Impressment in the armed forces was a further type of loss of freedom. The practice had medieval origins, but escalated sharply in the second half of the sixteenth century as conscript armies replaced feudal levies. Those drafted were in theory 'volunteers', but usually poor, as we know. And from Mary's reign officials made special efforts to send vagabonds on duty overseas. They scoured the streets, alehouses and bowling-alleys of London to catch 'recruits' in the 1590s, and again under James I and Charles I. Armies of the period sometimes numbered as many as 20,000 to 40,000 men, and since most were vagrants, many were obviously disposed of thus. They returned, however, to pester the country. And impressment was of dubious constitutionality. It was against the common law for foreign expeditions, but this obstacle was over-ridden by statute and commissions of array.

Vagrants also went overseas as 'indentured servants', though again under compulsion in many cases. The statutory authority arose from a provision in an Act of 1597; then in 1603 a Privy Council order also exiled rogues. In principle, offenders had the choice whether to go, but in practice the decision, as with impressment, was often made under duress. Some were even kidnapped from the streets. Large-scale transportations began under James I and continued at a high rate for the rest of the century. The total numbers sent are uncertain, but they surely ran into the thousands. They were mostly youngsters, whose lot was not necessarily much improved by the trip. In early Virginia they were treated as virtual slaves. Not surprisingly, the procedure sparked fear and resistance at home. In London in 1620 the poor and their children resisted, but the youths were despatched by Privy Council order just the same.

The bridewell, or house of correction, was perhaps the most revolutionary institution involving loss of freedom. With its aim

34

of reforming the idle, it prefigured later work-houses and modern prisons. The London Bridewell was chartered in 1553 and was followed by others in Gloucester, Ipswich and Norwich in the 1560s. Then after an Act of 1576 made them mandatory in all corporate towns, they proliferated and even spread abroad to the continent and to the New World. Bridewells sought to reform offenders by putting them to work, but penal elements were also present and in the end, perhaps inevitably in any lock-up, predominated. Most houses were indeed equipped to incarcerate and discipline their inmates: there were strong doors with locks, hand-cuffs, chains and irons. Prisoners were whipped for disobedience and swearing. Dress, diet and the daily routine were strictly regulated. In the Norwich Bridewell inmates worked from 5 am to 8 pm in summer and 6 am to 7 or 7.30 pm in winter. They were allotted half an hour to eat and 15 minutes to pray. Most provincial houses were small, a matter of one or two rooms, administered by a few officials. But London's had several rooms in 1631, and 30 officials, of whom 16 were to teach the prisoners trades. The bridewells grew in number in the seventeenth century after further statutes of 1597 and 1610 ordered their establishment.

Despite this expansion, it is doubtful whether the bridewells achieved their aim of making new persons of the poor. The houses suffered from a number of failings. Finance was one, for governments were usually unwilling or unable to commit the necessary funds to employ a substantial part of the unemployed population. Instead, administration was farmed out to contractors, whose salaries and resources were often pittances. The result was abuses. Contractors used the houses for private gain or neglected them. One even set up a brewery in the London Bridewell in 1600, and five years later another was running a brothel there, employing the prostitutes sent in for correction.

But perhaps the greatest difficulty was that those sent to bridewells were mainly offenders rather than the 'honest poor' in need of work. Over two-thirds of inmates in early seventeenth-century houses were malefactors of various kinds: vagrants, to be sure, but also unwed mothers and their bastard children, bigamists, drunkards, gamblers, scolds and slanderers, even prisoners of war.

At the end of the day, bridewell inmates simply reflected the wide scope of the legislation that incarcerated them. No wonder they developed the kind of problems associated with prisons: the mixing of bad and good inmates, with the first corrupting the second; fraternization of gaolers and prisoners; violence and brutality; escapes and rebellions. Once again, jurists had doubts about the legality of bridewells.

Conclusion

Governments devised a host of institutions in response to growing poverty from 1500 to 1650, which broadly speaking were the 'poor-laws'. But the legislation was a very large umbrella indeed. Its vagrancy clauses were chiefly concerned with the mainstay of the labour-force, those under masters, and with ensuring that they stayed in service. The Acts also covered a variety of 'deviant' occupational groups ranging from ballad-singers to unlicensed medicos, sexual offenders, even the transient minorities of gypsies and Irish. Poor-relief, for its part, became the law of the land. Like the vagrancy clauses of the poor-laws, it encompassed enormous changes in government, including secular parish administration and statutory taxation.

In the early nineteenth century William Cobbett proclaimed that 'the poor man in England is as secure from beggary as the King upon his Throne, because when he makes known his distress to the parish officers, they bestow upon him, not alms, but his legal dues'. Even in the mid-seventeenth century this assertion was substantially correct. This is not to say that the poor-laws were always justly and efficiently administered. The later abuses of the work-house and the Speenhamland system are too well known to make that sort of claim. Moreover, reformers eventually demanded changes in the laws, until finally the 'Old Poor Law' was abolished in 1834. And it is unlikely that the position of the poor was transformed by weekly doles and the rest, any more than that of today's is by social security payments. But for the ruling élites who instituted and administered the legislation, the poor-laws had positive results. They protected them from a host of disorders that might otherwise have threatened their social supremacy.

Bibliography

1 A. L. Beier, 'Vagrants and the Social Order in Elizabethan England', *Past and Present* 64 (1974).

2 A. L. Beier, 'The Social Problems of an Elizabethan Country Town: Warwick, 1580–90', in P. Clark (ed.), *Country Towns in Pre-Industrial England* (Leicester, 1981).

3 A. L. Beier, 'Poor-Relief in Warwickshire, 1630–1660', *Past and Present* 35 (1966).

4 P. Clark, 'The Migrant in Kentish Towns, 1580–1640', in P. Clark and P. Slack (eds), *Crisis and Order in English Towns, 1500–1700* (London, 1972).

5 D. C. Coleman, 'Labour in the English Economy of the Seventeenth Century', *Economic History Review*, 2nd series, VIII (1955–6).

6 G. R. Elton, 'An Early Tudor Poor-Law', *Economic History Review*, 2nd series, VI (1953).

7 R. N. Hadcock and D. Knowles, *Medieval Religious Houses, England and Wales* (London, 1971 edn).

8 J. F. Hadwin, 'Deflating Philanthropy', *Economic History Review*, 2nd series, XXXI (1978).

9 R. W. Herlan, 'Poor-Relief in London during the English Revolution', *Journal of British Studies* XVIII (1979).

10 W. G. Hoskins, *Provincial England* (London, 1963).

11 W. K. Jordan, *Philanthropy in England, 1480–1660* (London, 1959).

12 D. Knowles, *The Religious Orders in England* (Cambridge, 1959).

13 E. M. Leonard, *The Early History of English Poor-Relief* (Cambridge, 1900).

14 E. H. Phelps-Brown and S. V. Hopkins, 'Seven Centuries of the Prices of Consumables, Compared with Builders' Wage-Rates', *Economica* XXIII (1956).

15 J. F. Pound, *Poverty and Vagrancy in Tudor England* (London, 1971).

16 A. Savine, *English Monasteries on the Eve of the Dissolution* (Oxford Studies in Social and Legal History, 1909).

17 P. Slack, 'Poverty and Politics in Salisbury, 1597–1666', in P. Clark and P. Slack (eds), *Crisis and Order in English Towns, 1500–1700* (London, 1972).

18 P. Slack, 'Vagrants and Vagrancy in England, 1598–1664', *Economic History Review*, 2nd series, xxvii (1974).

19 *Statutes of the Realm* (London, 1819; London, 1963 edn), Vols i–iv.

20 R. H. Tawney, *Religion and the Rise of Capitalism* (London, 1926).

21 J. A. F. Thomson, 'Piety and Charity in Late Medieval London', *Journal of Ecclesiastical History* xvi (1965).

22 B. Tierney, *Medieval Poor-Law* (Berkeley, Calif., 1959).

23 S. and B. Webb, *English Poor-Law History. Part 1: The Old Poor Law* (London, 1927).

Appendix: Provisions of Tudor and Early Stuart poor-laws (19)

1495: *An Act Against Vagabonds and Beggars*
  1 States that laws of late fourteenth century are too rigorous and costly in treatment of vagabonds; provides for punishment in stocks rather than imprisonment;
  2 All disabled poor to return to home parishes, where they are allowed to beg, but not to leave their hundreds.

1531: *An Act Concerning Punishment of Beggars and Vagabonds*
  1 Provision for whipping of able-bodied beggars; complaint of rising numbers because of idleness;
  2 Disabled to be surveyed and licensed to beg by justices; if they leave area where licensed, to be whipped or placed in stocks.

1536: *An Act for Punishment of Sturdy Vagabonds and Beggars*
  1 Open doles to the poor to cease; the able to be put to continual labour; felony charges for persistent offenders;
  2 Voluntary alms to be collected by churchwardens or two others to relieve the disabled.

1547: *An Act for the Punishment of Vagabonds and for the Relief of the Poor and Impotent Persons*
  1 Possible enslavement of sturdy beggars for two years; for life if they ran away; offenders to be branded on the chest with a 'V';
  2 Cottages to be erected for the disabled and relief given to them;
  3 Weekly collections in the parish church after exhortation by a preacher.

1549: *An Act Touching the Punishment of Vagabonds and Other Idle Persons*
1 Repeal of vagrancy clauses of previous Act;
2 Re-enactment of provisions of 1547 concerning the disabled.

1552: *For the Provision and Relief of the Poor*
1 None to sit openly begging;
2 Local authorities and householders to nominate two collectors of alms for weekly collections on Sundays;
3 Persons refusing to contribute to be exhorted by ministers and then by bishops;
4 Records to be kept of names of the poor and contributors.

1563: *An Act for the Relief of the Poor*
1 Continues statutes of 1531 and 1549;
2 Persons refusing to contribute to poor-relief after being exhorted by a bishop to appear before justices with threat of possible imprisonment;
3 Fines of £2 for officials who neglect their poor-relief duties; £10 for refusing to be a collector; £20 for churchwardens who fail to report those unwilling to serve; £2 for ministers who neglect to announce elections for the position; imprisonment for collectors failing to produce quarterly accounts.

1572: *An Act for the Punishment of Vagabonds and for the Relief of the Poor and Impotent*
1 All convicted vagabonds above age 14 to be whipped and burned through the right ear unless some honest person takes them into service;
2 Felony charges for second and third offences;
3 Clauses relating to relief repeat 1552 and 1563 Acts;
4 Provision for persons who consider themselves over-taxed to appeal to Quarter Sessions;
5 Beggars' children aged from 5 to 14 may be bound out to service.

1576: *An Act for the Setting of the Poor on Work, and for the Avoiding of Idleness*
1 In every town officials to gather stocks of wool, etc., to set the poor to work;
2 Any persons refusing to work to be committed to a house of

correction, which are to be established in all counties and supported by rates.

1597: *An Act for the Relief of the Poor*
1 'Overseers of the poor' to be nominated in all parishes to employ the able poor, especially the young, and to administer relief;
2 Churchwardens and overseers empowered to distrain the goods of any persons refusing to contribute to poor-rates;
3 The same officials to see that habitations are provided for the disabled on waste or common lands, with the agreement of lords of manors;
4 County treasurers to be appointed to administer funds for the relief of prisoners and soldiers and mariners passing through the county.

1597: *An Act for the Punishment of Rogues, Vagabonds and Sturdy Beggars*
1 All previous Acts repealed;
2 Justices to see that houses of correction are erected in all counties and cities;
3 A new definition of vagrants, including as before the 'masterless' and dangerous occupations but also persons refusing to work for statutory wages;
4 Provision for incorrigible rogues to be sent overseas;
5 Convicted vagabonds to be whipped and returned to parishes of birth or last residence.

1604: *An Act for the Continuance and Explanation of the Statute Made in the 39th Year of the Reign of Our Late Queen Elizabeth, Entitled an Act For Punishment of Rogues, Vagabonds and Sturdy Beggars*
1 Provision for the branding of incorrigible rogues with an 'R' on their shoulders; felony charges for further offences;
2 All persons expected to apprehend vagrants upon pain of a 10s fine.

1610: *An Act for the Due Execution of Diverse Laws and Statutes Heretofore Made Against Rogues, Vagabonds and Sturdy Beggars and Other Lewd and Idle Persons*
1 Building of houses of correction has been neglected; to be erected in every county; fines for non-compliance;
2 Local officials to carry out searches for rogues at least twice yearly in all parishes;

41

3 Justices to commit mothers of bastard children to houses of correction for a year;
4 Persons who desert families shall be judged to be rogues.

NOTES

NOTES

NOTES

NOTES

NOTES

NOTES

NOTES

NOTES

NOTES

NOTES